Standing Watch

Grace Kotalik

STANDING WATCH

ISBN:9798332407093

DEDICATION

This book is dedicated to my brother and fallen hero, Jarrett.
And to my brother and active-duty U.S. Navy service member,
Noah.

STANDING WATCH

CONTENTS

FOREWORD

FOREWORD by Dr. Carl and Kim Ball, Gold Star Parents of U.S. Air Force Technical Sergeant, Cody William Ball

We met Grace soon after the passing of her brother, U.S. Army Specialist Jarrett Kotalik. We are Gold Star parents and we have become family friends. During this time, we have consistently witnessed Grace display qualities and values that are endearing and inspiring.

Grace is a highly motivated and responsible young woman. She consistently demonstrates a strong work ethic, taking initiative and completing tasks to a high standard, whether working independently or as part of a team. Her positive attitude and infectious enthusiasm are a source of inspiration to everyone she meets. She is always willing to go the extra mile, readily offering her help and support to others. We were so touched that she chose to honor our son, Cody, as part of her Eagle Project. Box #2 in the Collection bears his name.

Grace exemplified leadership potential throughout her Eagle project and we had several opportunities to observe her impact at dedication and retirement ceremonies. She demonstrated excellent organizational skills, effectively delegating tasks and motivating her team members. Her dedication and perseverance ensured the project's success, and it made a positive impact on Gold Star families while providing dignity for the American flag.

Grace possesses a strong moral compass. She is honest, trustworthy, and respectful towards others. Her empathy and compassion are evident in her interactions with everyone she meets. Her genuine desire to honor all fallen heroes will inspire you as she tells the story of her project, her plans for the future, all while facing her own unimaginable grief in *Standing Watch*.

1 THE CALL

July 10, 2023. 5:06 p.m.

My mom was in the kitchen, starting preparation for an early dinner.

Her phone rang.

My oldest brother, Noah, was calling her from his Navy base.

My mom hurried out of the room and quickly closed the bedroom door behind her.

"Mom. Jarrett is dead."

Those four words turned our world upside down in an instant.

2 THE NEXT DAY

I don't remember much about those first hours.

We were all in despair. Disbelief. And sad beyond words.

My parents arranged for a flight to get Noah home with us.

Hours later, a uniformed Army officer knocked at our door.

With Gold Star pins in hand, he delivered formal notice of Jarrett's death.

3 THE WHIRLWIND

The next couple of weeks were a blur.

Family friends delivered meals, words of comfort, and offered help.

Our family planned a local memorial service to honor Jarrett in our community.

Then, we traveled to Fort Liberty, North Carolina.

A different Army escort met us at the airport.

First, a unit service was planned.

Members of the 1-319 Field Artillery Regiment of the 82nd Airborne gathered to honor Jarrett. I stood between my brothers as each paratrooper paid their final respects and exited. We remained until we were the only ones left in the Chapel.

Then, a funeral.

I stood feeling numb as the 21-gun salute was carried out. I felt like each gun shot was being fired into my heart.

Last, a burial service.

Burying my beloved brother broke my heart.

I placed a stuffed bear, dressed in an Airborne uniform, in the niche of the Columbarium at the State Veteran's Cemetery along with his cremated remains. When the niche was closed, I felt like part of my heart was left in that cold, stone box.

4 THE LONG JOURNEY HOME

Our plane flight home was telling. A nightmare that would never end.

It was cancelled.

Then, we were rebooked on a flight.

We spent the night in the airport, waiting for a new flight, with no food or drink available for purchase.

It was in those hours that I realized life would never be the same again.

Holidays would be different. Family photos wouldn't include Jarrett's super cheese smile.

Gone was the brother who always made me laugh, the brother who would drive me crazy with his wild ideas, the brother who taught me to fish, the brother who was my student when I wanted to pretend, I was a teacher, and the brother who watched out for me.

My brother was gone WAY TOO SOON.

5 TURNING SADNESS INTO A TRIBUTE

The weeks after we returned to Texas from his services were a time of adjustment.

None of us were prepared for the change we were experiencing. We had so many questions. Even fewer answers. Each morning when I opened my eyes, I faced the same sad reality. He was gone.

I worried that Jarrett would be forgotten. And I decided that I couldn't let that happen.

I searched for ways to honor him in any way that I could.

6 FINDING STRENGTH

Each day, after July 10, 2023, was a challenge.

I had to realize that life isn't fair, and that Jarrett was gone.

I faced that every tomorrow would start without Jarrett and that I'd never hear his voice again.

I wasn't ready for Jarrett to be a memory.

I wanted him to walk in the door, with his big super cheese smile, and do anything to make me laugh again.

I looked for signs of Jarrett in everything- songs, places we had been, ponds we fished, sunsets (because fishing ends at sunset), Donald Duck, and the color blue.

I found strength when I held onto my memories of Jarrett.

I let those thoughts pull me through every day, even when the smallest things seemed impossible.

7 PLANNING AND DEVELOPING THE PROJECT

Following in the footsteps of Jarrett, my dad, and other brothers, I became a Life Scout in the Fall of 2023. As I began to consider ideas for my Eagle Scout project, I knew that I wanted it to be a tribute to Jarrett. Before his passing, he was a volunteer for our other brothers' Eagle projects. I realized that Jarrett wouldn't be "here" to help with mine.

My Scouting journey had become harder after Jarrett died because I had watched his path through Cub Scouts, bridging to a Troop, and becoming an Eagle Scout with Noah and Rafe. He had helped with part of my Scout adventures. I knew I needed to finish what I started, but there were days that I wondered whether I should put my journey on hold until I was better prepared to face this new reality.

Because Jarrett was deeply patriotic, I drew inspiration from him in my planning. After considering several different projects, I decided that a flag collection box and retirement ceremony would be the perfect project. I researched box designs and prepared my proposal.

I met with our District Advancement Chairperson. He is a Veteran and was familiar with our family's recent loss. He suggested that I expand my project idea into a flag box collection. He felt like it would expand the significance of my impact and I agreed.

8 MAKING IT BIGGER THAN I IMAGINED

Soon after he approved my proposal, I began the project planning phase.

Though my entire flag box collection would become a tribute to my brother Jarrett's devotion to honor veterans inspired me to memorialize other fallen heroes with special dedications.

Each of my ideas led to parts of a bigger picture. I continued to revise my designs, planning, and requested help from family, friends, and fellow Scouts.

I was touched by the outpouring of support for the project. Everyone seemed to understand why this was so important to me.

I never imagined that the project would blossom as it did.

9 THE SMALLEST OF DETAILS MATTER

Jarrett spent years as a Scout dedicated to serving our community and the surrounding area. He was an Eagle Scout, and he had a servant's heart. Some of our community's charitable organizations that benefitted from his efforts, over the years, included Interfaith of The Woodlands, Meals on Wheels of Montgomery County, the Rainbow Room, the Montgomery County Food Bank, Canopy Cancer Survivorship Center in The Woodlands, and several schools in Conroe Independent School District.

When Hurricane Harvey severely impacted our area, Jarrett helped at the local Red Cross shelter in South County with my other brothers. Jarrett had embraced service projects beyond our local area, for those who lost homes to flood and wildfire.

My initial concern was finding locations for the boxes that reflected his
philanthropy and commitment. It was comforting to connect with others who were eager to have a box placed at the locations that I planned.

Then, my energies shifted to designing the collection. With every aspect of the planning, I let my heart guide my decision-making. Because I wanted their stories shared around the world, I enlisted the help of my brother, Reed, to create a website to chronicle my project: flagboxesforfallenheroes.com.

My mom encouraged me to plan and develop each phase

just as I wanted, so I would have no regrets with the final outcome. And that's what I did.

10 DESIGNING & BUILDING THE FLAG BOX COLLECTION

The original collection included four flag boxes. I selected several design elements as reminders of Jarrett. The blue paint that I chose for the hinged lids was similar to Cubbie's Blue on the Chicago Cubs' uniforms, Jarret's favorite professional baseball team.

I would lead volunteers to hand paint 13 stripes around the sides of the boxes. While that is also the number of stripes on an American flag, Jarrett always connected that number to me because I was born on February 13. When he went through basic training, he wrote 213 inside his combat boots because he knew I was his cheering him on.

Each of the flag boxes has a silhouette painting on the front. I love to paint silhouettes as gifts to my family and the last one that I gave Jarrett depicted him catching a fish in the pond by our house.

Because Jarrett loved military history, each box in my collection has silhouettes of symbols related to United States memorials and significant locations that we visited as a family over the years.

Unique Design Elements of Box 1

The silhouette painting on the front of Box 1 depicts Jarrett after landing in the drop zone at Fort Liberty, North Carolina (formerly known as Fort Bragg).

The illustration on the side panel depicts paratroopers making a jump. Jarrett's lifelong dream was to earn his wings and serve as a member of the United States Airborne. At 18 years and 1 day of age, he did what he set out to do and the iconic parachutist badge was pinned on his uniform. He recorded 20 jumps before he passed away. Our family arranged for a 21st ceremonial jump when we were at the base for his memorial services.

Unique Design Elements of Box 2

The silhouette painting on the front of Box 2 is U.S. Air Force Technical Sergeant Cody Ball looking at jets in the sky.

The illustrations on the side panel of jets flying above the mountains reminds me of family trips to Colorado Springs, home of the U.S. Air Force Academy. The Space Force is a new branch in the Armed Services that is organized under the Air Force. The space shuttle is a reflection of family trips to the Houston Space

Center, Smithsonian's National Air and Space Museum, and Kennedy Space Center.

Unique Design Elements of Box 3

The silhouette painting on the front of Box 3 depicts U.S.

Army Specialist Joey Lenz honorably serving our great nation.

The illustrations on the side panel symbolize the Vietnam Veterans Memorial in Washington, D.C. and National Battlefields across the United States. Jarrett visited "The Wall" and several battlefields with our family, including Vicksburg, Pea Ridge, Manassas, Valley Forge, Gettysburg, and Fort McHenry.

Unique Design Elements of Box 4

The silhouette painting on the front of Box 4 depicts U.S. Navy HM1 Kristofer Guy and U.S. Marine Lance Corporal Armando Hernandez honorably serving our great nation.

The illustrations on the side panel of marines lifting a flag reminds me of family trips to Washington, D.C. to see the U.S. Marine Corps War Memorial. The second image is a naval ship. Jarrett and my brothers have visited and stayed overnight on several, including the USS Lexington and the USS Kidd. As a family, we have toured the USS Texas, USS Alabama, USS Constitution and USS Constellation. Now, our oldest brother Noah is in the U.S. Navy, assigned to a destroyer in the Pacific Fleet.

11 SHARING STORIES OF THE FALLEN

Following Jarrett's passing, I met other Gold Star families. Like us, they lost their loved ones in active service. I listened to their stories. It became important to me that I include their loved one as part of my project. I felt like Jarrett would want me to do that.

BOX ONE- Located at Trinity Episcopal Church, Butler Hall, 3901 S. Panther Creek Dr., The Woodlands, Texas

Date of Dedication- February 1, 2024

Box 1 in the collection was designed in memory of my brother, U.S. Army Specialist Jarrett Kotalik. Once the box was

built by Scouts and volunteers under my leadership, I held a dedication ceremony to unveil it. At that time, my brother Rafe shared this tribute to Jarrett.

"To know Jarrett was to love Jarrett. He lived for adventure and hated to just sit around. He loved baseball, hockey, football, motorsports, and watching our youngest brother, Reed, play lacrosse. Jarrett was fearless and adventurous. He spent years as a Boy Scout dedicated in service to The Woodlands and surrounding communities. He joined Cub Scouting in elementary school and earned his Arrow of Light as a member of Pack 777 here at Trinity Episcopal. He bridged to become a Boy Scout in 2013. He attended camps with me and Noah, and other Scout friends. Jarrett, Noah, and I became Eagle Scouts on April 18, 2018. We were determined to do that together. We
shared so many Scouting adventures, including our time spent carving a Snofa together at Northern Tier."

"Jarrett was always ready to assist service projects. He had a servant's heart and supported many of my lofty ideas, even when others would suggest that my goal were too large. If I was wanting to help wildfire survivors in California, hurricane victims in Louisiana, those affected by floods in Tennessee or Nebraska, Jarrett's question was never "why," it was how much do you want to do and how can I help you?"

"My favorite memories with Jarrett will be on the hikes at Gettysburg, Manassas, and around our U.S. Capitol with him and our dad. Even once Jarrett left for bootcamp and my dad and I returned for hikes in those areas, we always took Jarrett's Union cap with us, and we would hold it in our photos, so we kept him with us "in spirit.""

"Jarrett's desire to join the military and serve in the 82nd Airborne Division began in elementary school. Our great grandfather was a paratrooper during the Normandy invasion in World War II."

"Jarrett loved our family travels that included overnight stays on the USS Kidd and Battleship Texas. He took advantage of any opportunity to run around aircraft carriers, submarines, or climb on canons at National Battlefields."

"Jarrett worked hard to graduate, ahead of schedule, from high school so that he could enlist in the Army as a 17-year-old. He was determined to serve our country and chart his own military career path. After basic combat training at Fort Jackson, South Carolina, he successfully completed advanced training as a Fire Control Specialist at Fort Sill, Oklahoma just before the start of the COVID pandemic. On his 18th birthday he was jumping from perfectly good airplanes to earn his wings. After Airborne school at Fort Benning, Georgia, he was transferred to his duty station at the Home of the 82nd Airborne Division where he served until his unexpected passing at the age of 21. During his almost 4 years of service, he earned several awards and commendations, including the Good Conduct Medal, National Defense Service Medal, Military Outstanding
Volunteer Service Medal, Army Commendation Medal, Global War on Terrorism Service Medal, Army Service Ribbon, Parachutist Badge, and a Marksmanship Badge."

"Jarrett's hobbies included fishing and hunting. He cast his line into streams, rivers, and lakes in many ponds around The Woodlands, in the Ozarks, Swamp regions in Louisiana, and most recently in North Carolina and Maryland."

"As our family looks to the future, we will all picture Jarrett with his signature "super cheese" smile and perched up in the clouds. He will be dangling his feet, casting his line, and looking down with a fishing pole in hand to tell us that he has our backs. He will live on FOREVER in our hearts."

BOX TWO- Originally located at South County Community Center, 2235 Lake Robbins Drive, The Woodlands,

Texas

Date of Dedication- January 26, 2024

Relocated after Presentation to the Montgomery County Commissioner's Court to Central Library, Montgomery County Memorial Library System (adjacent to Montgomery County Veteran's Memorial Park) 104 Interstate 45 N, Conroe, Texas

Date of Relocation- February 6, 2024

I chose to dedicate Box 2 of my flag box collection in memory of Technical Sergeant Cody William Ball and Other Fallen Heroes of the United States Air Force. Once the box was built by Scouts and volunteers under my leadership, I planned a dedication ceremony and shared Cody's story.

From the family of U.S. Air Force Technical Sergeant Cody Ball:

"Cody was born in Topeka, Kansas on May 15, 1991. He had a childhood full of adventure. He loved playing outside with his friends, his big sister, riding his big wheel, playing with his dog, and going fishing. Cody was a typical boy, he liked getting dirty, trucks, Legos, airplanes, and engines. Cody was always a kind, loving, funny guy, and above all he was a momma's boy. He was at his mom's side from the time he was born until he left for boot camp.

He loved and adored his mom and she loved and adored him. Those who knew him rarely saw him without a smile on his face. He didn't stay mad or hold grudges. He was always laughing and playing practical jokes. He had a great laugh and bright smile. When he loved, he loved hard. Cody loved to travel and was always up to seeing new places, he wanted to see the world. Following in his father's footsteps, he joined the military."

"He participated in Army JROTC while he was in high school. When he graduated, he enlisted in the Air Force. His first day of active duty on September 1, 2009. Coincidentally, this was his father's first day of retirement from active duty. His mom got one back and sent one off on the same day."

"He graduated from boot camp on his mom's birthday and then went on to tech school in Wichita Falls, Texas. Upon completion of tech school, he became an Aerospace Propulsion Specialist. His first duty station was in Japan where he served 4 years advancing to the rank of Sergeant. His next duty station was in North Carolina where he served 4 years advancing to the rank of Staff Sergeant. His final duty station was in the United Kingdom. He was a member of the 492nd Fighter Generation Squadron "Mad Hatters." While stationed there he found his stride, he was Airman of the quarter twice, Airman of the Year and Maintainer of the Year. He advanced to Technical Sergeant while he was there. He served on active duty for 13.5 years. The squadron dedicated a special F-15 in his honor. F-15 tail number LN AF98134 will carry his name forever."

"His fellow Airman repeatedly said he was the morale of the command and always kept the aircraft flying. He was considered the "go to" guy when it came to his job, affectionately known as the "Engine God." He was known as a great leader, mentor, and most of all a great friend. Cody was a great son, father, brother, airman and is missed dearly and never forgotten."

Since the time of dedication, families of other U.S. Air Force fallen heroes have shared their stories with me and I have added them to the project's website.

BOX 3- Located at Interfaith of The Woodlands, 4242 Interfaith Way, The Woodlands, Texas

Date of Dedication- January 31, 2024

I chose to dedicate Box 3 of my flag box collection in memory of Specialist Joey Lenz and Other Fallen Heroes of the United States Army. Once the box was built by Scouts and volunteers under my leadership, I planned a dedication ceremony

and shared Joey's story.

From the family of U.S. Army Specialist Joey Lenz:

"Joey Lenz was born November 16,1989, in Baytown, Texas. Joey was the youngest of their three sons. Specialist Lenz enlisted in the Army on September 18, 2017, completed Basic Combat Training at Fort Jackson, South Carolina on December 4, 2017, and Advanced Individual Training as a 91D Generator Mechanic at Fort Lee, Virginia on March 7, 2018."

"He was deployed to the Republic of Korea October 2019 through February 2021 where he served as a Tactical Power Generator Specialist. As a generator mechanic he received many accolades including the National Defense Service Medal, Korea Defense Service Medal, Army Service Ribbon, and the Overseas Service Ribbon."

"Specialist Lenz displayed tireless devotion in support of the Echo Forward Support Company, 3rd Brigade Engineer Battalion. He contributed significantly to the Battalion. Specialist Lenz assisted in scheduled and unscheduled maintenance operations. His ability to adapt demonstrated a pattern of outstanding performance while conducting monthly scheduled services and unscheduled repairs."

"Through his exceptional meritorious service, Lenz distinguished himself by demonstrating to all that he was a professional Soldier, dedicated to excellence in his field of expertise. His untiring efforts and can-do attitude attest to his achievements and accolades as an outstanding Soldier. SPC Lenz's ability to adapt to his team while providing maintenance support was critical during the rotation in South Korea."

"Specialist Joey Lenz was awarded an Honorary Award for exceptionally meritorious service while assigned as a Power Generation Mechanic. His service and dedication were an integral part of the unit's overall success. Lenz was an enthusiastic, caring, and kind young man known for his deep passion of all animals especially cats and dogs. His humor was contagious, and he never met a stranger. Some people make your laugh a little louder, your smile a little brighter, and your life a little better. Joey was loved by soldiers, good friends, and family. He made our life better!"

Since the time of dedication, families of other U.S. Army fallen heroes have shared their stories with me and I have added them to the project's website.

BOX 4- Located at Timber Lakes Timber Ridge HOA, 25610 Timber Lakes Drive, Spring, Texas

Date of Dedication- January 30, 2024

I chose to dedicate Box 4 of my flag box collection in memory of Fallen Heroes of the United States Navy and Marines. Once the box was built by Scouts and volunteers under my leadership, I planned a dedication ceremony and shared Kris and Armando's stories.

From the family of U.S. Navy PO1 Kristofer Guy:

"PO1 Kristofer Guy joined the United States Navy on January 3,1997 and completed his duty for the Navy and on this earth on March 3, 2015. Kris comes from a long line of Sailors; as his Dad served in Vietnam, his maternal grandfather in Korea, paternal grandfather in World War II and he had an Uncle who served both in Korea and Vietnam. All were sailors. He served the Navy and United States with honor, courage, and commitment. One of his shipmates characterized him as the epitome of the Navy saying, "Ship, Shipmate, and Self." His last duty and duty station was as LPO for the Radiology Department at Naval Medical Center Portsmouth in Virginia. During his time in the Navy, he developed many friendships. Many of those friends still pay tribute to him when the opportunity arises. He was loved and respected by all who knew him and enjoyed his unique sense of humor."

"Kris left behind a large loving family including his wife and twins. Kris' presence while alive was large and in death, he has left a void in the universe that can never be filled. Fair Winds and Following Seas, Doc."

From the family of U.S. Marine Lance Corporal Armando Hernandez:

"Lance Corporal Armando Hernandez left to bootcamp in San Diego, CA August 12, 2019, and graduated November 8, 2019. He spent a month in Camp Pendleton, CA conducting Marine Combat Training and moved to the Army Quartermaster School in Fort Lee, Virginia. In July of 2020 he received orders to Okinawa, Japan after completing initial Electro-Optical Repair School and reported to 3d Maintenance Battalion, 3d Marine Logistics Group and was assigned to Ordnance Repair Platoon."

"While assigned to Ordinance Maintenance, Lance

Corporal Hernandez conducted multiple operational and training events. Some of the most notable was Jungle Warfare Training, Lance Corporal's Leadership and Ethics Seminar, Helicopter Egress training along with many Company, Battalion, and Field Training Events."

mention the love for his family and friends. His genuine heart along with the combination of his calm quiet presence, his steady demeanor, and his can-do attitude won him many loyal and faithful friends. Armando was wise beyond his years and would light up the room with his interesting character. Armando made a home of the barracks and was the glue who kept the Marines together. He celebrated holidays and birthdays for the boys on base and cooked homemade recipes to make a home away from home for them. Lance Corporal Hernandez passed away in an accident on base while on active duty. He is loved by many and will be missed."

Since the time of dedication, families of other U.S. Navy and Marine fallen heroes have shared their stories with me, and I have added them to the project's website.

BOX 5- Located at South County Community Center, 2235 Lake Robbins Drive, The Woodlands, Texas

Date of Delivery- March 20, 2024

The project plan was a four-box collection. After the dedication of Box 2, I was invited to speak before the Commissioner's Court. I was told that County officials wanted to relocate that box so that it was adjacent to the large Veteran's Memorial Park in our community. I was honored by the invitation and agreed to move the box.

However, I was also saddened to remove it from the South

County Community Center because Jarrett was involved in several projects that benefited the seniors served at that facility. I decided that I should use wood, remaining from my project, to make a fifth, slightly smaller box to replace Box 2.

Box 5 would be to honor all fallen heroes, regardless of branch of service. The silhouette painting on the front would depict Jarrett, Cody, and Kris together.

The painted images on the five-box collection were designed to serve as a reminder that our fallen heroes were watching over the symbol of our Nation until proper retirement.

12 GATHERING FLAGS & PLANNING THE FLAG RETIREMENT CEREMONY

Once the boxes were delivered and dedicated, they quickly filled with flags. I had Reed create a QR code for the collection. Each time that flags were placed inside, visitors completed a form that alerted me. I arranged pick up of the donated flags. I led Scouts to continue preparation of them for a large United States Flag Retirement Ceremony. I also received flags from a box placed at Honor Café in Conroe, Texas by the Spring Creek Area TX 18 Blue Star Mothers of America, Inc.

When I visited local Veterans of Foreign War and American Legion posts to share details about my project, I was given additional flags to retire. Members of a Houston-area post traveled to meet me at Trinity. They presented me with boxes of large American Flags, flown over Reliant Stadium, which were sun-faded and worn.

I am forever grateful to all those who helped during the service events to inspect, fold, and prepare the flags for retirement.

13 EIGHTY PAGES IN MEMORIAM

When it came time to plan the large flag retirement ceremony, I knew that I wanted it to be a memorable tribute. I spent hours reading stories of our Nation's fallen heroes. Some were killed in action or died in other traumatic events. Others died of illness. There are those who died in foreign lands and many who passed at bases in our country, like Jarrett.

I found myself wanting to honor them all. I started writing a script for my volunteers. After nearly a month, it became an 80-page memoriam.

March 9th was fast approaching. I visited the ceremony site for a final walk-through of my plan. The backdrop for the Outdoor Amphitheater at BSA Camp Strake is a lake front. There is a fishing pier that is often used by Scouts. Since Jarrett loved to fish, it was the perfect spot for this tribute.

I recruited members of my troop, our linked boys' troop, and Cub Scout pack to assist. Some had speaking roles, others would be flag bearers and assist with set up and clean up, and some would help at the main gate with check-in. All would have a vital role in honoring our fallen American heroes.

On the day of the Ceremony, the sky was clear, and it was windy. The local Coldspring Volunteer Fire Department agreed to assist with fire watch and standby with trucks as needed. As the ceremony guests took their seats at the amphitheater, I noticed many Veterans of different branches and conflicts seated in the audience.

As we took our places behind the stage, grey fog rolled onto the stage from machines. I wanted the introduction to resemble the ceremony at Fort Jackson, South Carolina on January 16, 2020, when Jarrett graduated from Basic Training. My brother, Reed, played the beginning of Promentory from Last of the Mohicans. Then, I said (from backstage on a microphone): "For the warriors who fight and die so the rest of us may fight to live." Reed faded Promentory and started the song "Soldiers" by Otherwise. As the music played, I walked to the podium with my Scout friend, Emilia. As other Scouts unfurled and stood with a large, American flag, I shared a message about its meaning.

I described the flag as a banner of hope for generations of Americans following its' birth on June 14, 1777. 1777 is also the number for my Troop. I explained our Flag's history, the significance of its design, symbolism for our Armed Forces, and that it has been placed into the hands of too many families (like mine) who have lost loved ones who died in service to our great nation.

Then, I told of the honorable way that we retire and replace flags so they may continue to symbolize our Country.

The audience stood with me and the other Scouts to recite the Pledge of Allegiance. Afterwards, the Scouts exited, and I made other introductions before we commenced with retiring hundreds of tattered flags.

Prior to this Ceremony, the flags were inspected by more than 30 volunteers that I had recruited since Veteran's Day 2023. During that inspection, these flags to be retired were found to be no longer suitable for display. Fresh new Flags now fly in their place.

I shared the story of my Eagle project. I paid tribute to Jarrett's influence on the meaning of my efforts. I told the story of my project's development, from design and building of the boxes. I described the delivery of them and dedication ceremonies.

At that time, the first of several Gold Star families were invited to the stage. U.S. Air Force Technical Sergeant Cody W. Ball's mom carried a photo of him. His dad, an Air Force and Coast Guard Veteran himself, handed a worn American flag to one of the Scout bearers so that it could be placed into the fire ring. As **Flag #1** turned to ashes, Emilia shared Cody's story. Then, his parents returned to their seats.

Two Scout flag bearers came to the stage, holding more folded cloths of our Country. As Emilia shared the stories of U.S. Navy PO1 Kristopher L. Guy and U.S. Marine Lance Corporal Armando Hernandez, Nikhil and Vikram placed **Flags #2 and #3** into the fire rings. We paused until the stars and stripes were no longer visible in the flames.

Next, U.S. Army Specialist Joey Lenz's family was invited to the stage. The audience viewed a photo of Joey and heard his story, as **Flag #4** was retired in his honor. Afterwards, his family returned to their seats in the Gold Star Family section.

Flag #5 was in remembrance of Jarrett. Once my family stepped on stage, my brother Rafe approached the microphone. He shared Jarrett's eulogy as he did at the dedication ceremony on February 1st. My mom held a photo of Jarrett, and my dad handed the flag a Scout flag bearer to place into the fire ring. I was nearly overwhelmed with sadness as I watched it turn into ashes.

Emilia stepped in and asked all the Gold Star families in attendance to rise.

Once they did, she said, "You have given so much; this ceremony seems inadequate compared to your family's loss. Grace hopes her project will serve as a reminder that your son or daughter's passing was not in vain. They will never be forgotten and in years to come, everyone who visits the flag boxes will be reminded of their stories. Those who place flags to be retired in them, will see the paintings, and they will know that your hero continues to be watching over the symbol of our Nation until the flags can be properly retired. Thank you for your continued service to our military and Veterans and for being a reminder to us as to the sacrifice made by your son or daughter."

Then, the families were seated.

I stepped to the microphone again and said, "As a Gold Star sister, I can tell you that it is always comforting when our fallen heroes are remembered and honored. As we retire American flags today, I want to honor the legacy and lives of the fallen by saying their names. As each flag is placed into one of our two flag rings, Emilia and I will say their names and honor hundreds of fallen heroes in our Armed Forces."

Next, Scout volunteers prepared 401 additional flags for retirement. Our reading of names commenced with Section II of the Flag Retirement Ceremony. We shared some stories that had been offered by the families of these fallen heroes.

Flag #6- U.S. Air Force Airman 1st Class Michael Mahony, of The Woodlands, was based at the Royal Air Force Base, Lakenheath, England. He died on Christmas Day 2018.

Michael's family has said, "he was mischievous, funny, thrill seeking, and loyal to the core to family, friends, and country."

"He was loved by all and truly never met a stranger, seriously, that kid would talk to anyone and make instant lifelong friends. His compassion was deep, and his love was strong. This world was a better place with Michael in it, he will be forever missed. May He Never Be forgotten!"

Flag #7- U.S. Army Staff Sergeant Gary Lee Woods Jr., of Lebanon Junction, Kentucky, died on April 10, 2009, in service during Operation Iraqi Freedom. His family said, "he was a fine soldier who will be remembered for cracking jokes to help others through tense situations and for his love of music. He was awarded for his bravery with the Bronze Star, Medal of Valor, and Purple Heart."

Flag #8- U.S. Army Corporal Brandon Smitherman, of Conroe, Texas was assigned to the 2nd Battalion, 7th Calvary Regiment, 4th Brigade Combat Team, 1st Calvary Division, in Fort Bliss, Texas. His family shared that "Brandon died on October 31, 2007, in Iraq from injuries sustained when an explosive device detonated near his vehicle during combat operations. Corporal Smitherman was awarded the Bronze Star Medal and Purple Heart for his bravery on the battlefield. Smitherman, who was often referred to as "Smitty" by his fellow soldiers, earned the nickname "Little Tim" because he drove a Bradley fighting vehicle for Captain Timothy McGovern, the unit's commander who became Smitherman's mentor. Army Brigadier General Francis C. Mahon said at the funeral that Brandon was picked to be Captain McGovern's driver because of his outstanding performance as a soldier."

"Friends and former teachers have said that Smitherman was a compassionate young man whose smile touched everyone he met. Smitherman enjoyed sports, excelling in football and basketball. He played as a defensive end for the Montgomery High School Bears."

"Smitherman was willing to assist everyone he met, friends said – to comfort an emotional school bus driver after she hit a dog, to help arrange the engagement of a fellow soldier and to protect the freedoms of a nation. Perhaps the words scrawled on homemade signs held by the hundreds of strangers lining Conroe streets thanking Smitherman for his sacrifice were the most telling about the message he left behind. "Home of the free because of the brave."

Next, I invited the family of U.S. Army Private First Class Matthew Guyon to come forward. Matthew's mom stood before our audience as she held a photograph of him. As his dad handed Scout bearers **Flag #9** to be retired in Matthew's honor, I shared the following story provided by his family.

Private First Class Matthew Guyon, of LaPorte, Texas, was stationed at Ft. Carson, Colorado when he tragically passed away on June 4th, 2020. Matthew was an active volunteer growing up. He received multiple Presidential Volunteer Service awards including the Gold award. He was co-recipient of the American Red Cross Rising Star award. He volunteered with The La Porte Police Department's Explorers, The Office of Emergency Management, The La Porte Animal Shelter, The Community Emergency Response Team, Pipefitters Local Union 211, and more."

"Matthew was always thinking of others, and he had a passion for cooking. He was incredibly excited to enter the Army as a cook and was invited to join their competition culinary team. His passion was BBQ. He loved to gather with friends and coworkers for a BBQ. His best friends from home, Korbin, Chris, and Isaiah will always cherish the memories they built together. Matthew lived life to its fullest and had fallen in love with the awe of Colorado. When he wasn't at work he could likely be found surrounded by God's beauty in the nearby mountains. His daily texts of how much he loved his mama and daddy will be missed always as well as his dry sense of humor and his passion to always be the best! He was an amazing person! He always put others first and while the world will be a little bit dimmer without his beautiful light here, his happiness was contagious, and that joy-filled smile will live on always."

Flag #10 was retired in memory of U.S. Army Sergeant First Class Adam J. Donaldson, of Glen Burnie, Maryland, died November 15, 2021. As the flag was placed into the fire ring, Emilia shared his story, as provided by his family.

"Adam graduated from Glen Burnie Senior High School in 2002 and at the age of 18, set his sights on serving in the United States Army. During his 19 years of service, Adam completed tours in Korea, Germany, Iraq, and Poland. Adam was a skilled mechanic, and he became known during a battalion "Able Call" ceremony as the "Tank Whisperer," by other senior leader belt buckle holders. This award is given to you for being known, within the ranks, for how to be proficient at your job. Prior to his passing, Adam enjoyed spending time with his kids and family. He loved to grill and go mudding in his jeep. He is dearly missed by all those who had an opportunity to be in his presence."

Flag #11 was burned in tribute to U.S. Marine Corporal Kyle Martin Stout died on August 13, 2018, in South Carolina. His family said, "he was stationed at Paris Island and served in Provost Marshall Office. At the time, he was the youngest Marine to be selected for the Special Reaction Teams. He loved the Marines and Paris Island. He once told his mom that if he could stay stationed there forever, he would. It's where he was happiest. Kyle's passions were cars, ice hockey, the Marines and his little girl, Lizzy."

I invited the mother of U.S. Army Private First-Class Trent J. Fontenot to come forward. She stood before our audience as she held a photograph of him, and she spoke about her son's legacy. **Flag #12** was handed to Scout bearers to be retired in Trent's honor; honorable U.S. soldier who died while serving in Operation Desert Storm. This is the story that she shared:

"PFC Trent Joseph Fontenot was born in Weisbaden Germany, July 5, 1971, while his father was on active duty. He died in service, pending deployment to Operation Desert Storm on March 3, 1991 at Ft. Hood, Texas. He was well loved by his fellow soldiers, some of them are still in contact with our family. Trent was proud of his family's military service to our country. His paternal great grandfather served in World War I; his grandfather served in World War II in France using his Creole French as a translator; his father is a retired Lieutenant Colonel, US Army, having served in Vietnam. Additionally, Trent had a maternal grandfather, who served in the US Navy, Sergeant Nolan Jackson Sr., during World War II, and two uncles who were Vietnam era military service members: First-Class Petty Officer, Tony Jackson, US Navy and Technical Sergent, Kenneth Jackson, US Air Force."

Flag #13 was retired in tribute to U.S. Army Chief Petty Officer Peter J. Hundahl who died May 25, 2020 because of Agent Orange Complications. "He was my hero, and I miss him so much," said his mother, Barbara Hundahl.

Following a brief intermission to check the safety of the fire rings, we began with the presentation of Section III of the Flag Retirement Ceremony.

Section III
Flags 14-16
Senior Airman Bradley R. Smith, United States Air Force
Staff Sergeant Seth Micheal Plant, United States Army
Specialist Micheal Demarsico, United States Army

Flags 17-19
Private First-Class Vincent Ellis, United States Army
Sergeant Adam Ray, United States Army
Private First-Class Kenneth Zeigler II United States Army

Flags 20-22
Hospital Corpsman 3 Athan Allen, United States Navy
Staff Sergeant Daniel Wadham, United States Army
Gunnery Sergeant Justin Martone, United States Marine
Corps

Flags 23-25
Corporal Matthew Winkler, United States Army
Airman First Class Kyle Truitt, United States Air Force
Petty Officer 3 Paul Stock III, United States Navy

Flags 26-28
Sergeant Garrett Mongrella, United States Army
Specialist Joseph Lancour, United States Army
Private Joshua Dommes, United States Army

Flags 29-31
Specialist Joseph Lucas, United States Army
Specialist Patrick Tillman, United States Army
Private First-Class Justin Dreese, United States Army

Flags 32-34
Sergeant Aaron Blasjo, United States Army
Lance Corporal Anthony Melia, United States Marine
Corps
Specialist Tyler Cameron Blair, United States Army

Flags 35-37
Sergeant Zachary Fisher, United States Army
Corporal Mick Bekowsky, United States Marine Corps
Sergeant William Rivers, United States Army

Flags 38-40
Specialist Kennedy Sanders, United States Army
Specialist Breonna Moffett, United States Army
Special Warfare Operator, 1st Class Christopher

Chambers, United States Navy

Flags 41-43
Special Warfare Operator 2nd Class Nathan Ingram,
United States Navy
Staff Sergeant James Alford, United States Army
Major Shawn Campbell, United States Marine Corps

Flags 44-46
Corporal William Taylor, United States Marine Corps
Sergeant Ryan Curtis, United States Marine Corps
Sergeant Major James Sartor, United States Army

Flags 47-49
Staff Sergeant Darin Hoover, United States Marine Corps
Sergeant Johanny Rosario Pichardo, United States Marine
Corps
Sergeant Nicole L. Gee, United States Marine Corps

Flags 50-52
Corporal Hunter Lopez, United States Marine Corps
Corporal Daegan W. Page, United States Marine Corps
Corporal Humberto A. Sanchez, United States Marine
Corps

Following a brief intermission to check the safety of the
fire rings, we began with the presentation of Section IV of the
Flag Retirement Ceremony.

Section IV
    Flags 53-55
    Lance Corporal David L. Espinoza, United States Marine
    Corps
    Lance Corporal Jared M. Schmitz, United States Marine
    Corps
    Lance Corporal Rylee J. McCollum, United States Marine
    Corps

Flags 56-58
Staff Sergeant Ryan C. Knauss, United States Army
Private First Class Corey Kosters, United States Army
Corporal Zachary Endsley, United States Army

Flags 59-61
Lance Corporal Dylan R. Merola, United States Marine Corps
Lance Corporal Kareem M. Nikou, United States Marine Corps
Hospital Corpsman Maxton W. Soviak, United States Navy

Flags 62-64
Sergeant First Class Javier Gutierrez, United States Air Force
Sergeant First Class Antonio Rodriguez, United States Army
Staff Sergeant Ian McLaughlin, United States Army

Flags 65-67
Corporal Robert Drawl, Jr., United States Army
Sergeant Wakkuna Jackson, United States Army
Senior Airman Adam P. Servais, United States Air Force

Flags 68-70
Specialist Christopher F. Sitton, United States Army
Private Joseph R. Blake, United States Army
Corporal Jeremiah S. Cole, United States Army

Flags 71-73
Specialist Rogelio R. Garza, Jr., United States Army
Private First-Class Andrew R. Small, United States Army
Private First-Class James P. White, Jr., United States Army

Flags 74-76

Staff Sergeant Daniel A. Suplee, United States Army
Specialist Andrew Velez, United States Army
Sergeant David M. Hierholzer, United States Army

Flags 77-79
First Sergeant Christopher C. Rafferty, United States Army
Staff Sergeant Eric Caban, United States Army
Staff Sergeant Robert J. Chiomento, United States Army

Flags 80-82
Sergeant Robert P. Kassin, United States Army
Private First-Class Kevin F. Edgin, United States Army
Sergeant Major Jeffrey A. McLochlin, United States Army

Flags 83-85
Chief Warrant Officer 3 William T. Flanigan, United States Army
Private First-Class Justin R. Davis, United States Army
Staff Sergeant Joseph F. Fuerst III, United States Army

Flags 86-88
Master Sergeant Thomas D. Maholic, United States Army
Private First-Class Brian J. Bradbury, United States Army
Staff Sergeant Heathe N. Craig, United States Army

Flags 89-91
Staff Sergeant Patrick L. Lybert, United States Army
Sergeant 1st Class Jared C. Monti, United States Army
1st Lieutenant Forrest P. Ewens, United States Army

Flags 92-94
Sergeant Ian T. Sanchez, United States Army
Commanding Officer Patrick D. Damon, United States Army
Sergeant Roger P. Pena, Jr., United States Army

Flags 95-97

Sergeant Russell M. Durgin, United States Army
Lieutenant Colonel Charles E. Munier, United States Army
Corporal Bernard P. Corpuz, United States Army

Flags 98-100
Specialist Curtis R. Mehrer, United States Army
Sergeant Travis A. Vanzoest, United States Army
Corporal Derek A. Stanley, United States Army

Following a brief intermission to check the safety of the fire rings, we began with the presentation of Section V of the Flag Retirement Ceremony.

Section V
Flags 101-103
Staff Sergeant Christian Longsworth, United States Army
Sergeant Bryan A. Brewster, United States Army
Chief Warrant Officer 2 Christopher B. Donaldson, United States Army

Flags 104-106
Lieutenant Colonel Joseph J. Fenty, United States Army
Sergeant John C. Griffith, United States Army
Staff Sergeant Christopher T. Howick, United States Army
Flags 107-109
Private First-Class Brian M. Moquin, Jr., United States Army
Specialist Justin L. O'Donohoe, United States Army
Specialist David N. Timmons, Jr., United States Army

Flags 110-112
Chief Warrant Officer 3 Eric W. Totten, United States Army
Sergeant Jeffery S. Wiekamp, United States Army
Captain Clayton L. Adamkavicius, United States Army

Flags 113-115

Sergeant 1st Class John T. Stone, United States Army
Staff Sergeant Christopher L. Robinson, United States Army
Lance Corporal Nicholas R. Anderson, United States Marine Corps

Flags 116-118
Specialist Zachary Scott Reiss, US Army Reserves
Corporal Nathaniel Farsdale, United States Marine Corps
Sergeant First Class Matthew Q. McClintock, United States Army

Flags 119-121
Sergeant Kevin D. Akins, United States Army
Sergeant Anton J. Hiett, United States Army
Sergeant Joshua L. Hill, United States Army

Flags 120-122
Staff Sergeant Joseph R. Ray, United States Army
Master Sergeant Emigdio E. Elizarraras, United States Army
1st Lieutenant Brandon R. Dronet, United States Marine Corps

Flags 123-125
Sergeant James F. Fordyce, United States Marine Corps
Senior Airman Alecia S. Good, United States Air Force
Lance Corporal Samuel W. Large, Jr., United States Marine Corps

Flags 126-128
Sergeant Donnie Leo F. Levens, United States Marine Corps
Corporal Matthieu Marcellus, United States Marine Corps
Sergeant Jonathan E. McColley, United States Marine Corps

Flags 129-131
Staff Sergeant Luis M. Melendez-Sanchez, United States Air Force
Lance Corporal Nicholas J. Sovie, United States Marine Corps
Captain Bryan D. Willard, United States Marine Corps
Flags 132-134
Staff Sgt. Edwin H. Dazachacon, United States Army
Sgt. 1st Class Chad A. Gonsalves, United States Army
Sgt. Alberto D. Montrond, United States Army

Flags 135-137
Staff Sgt. Clinton T. Newman, United States Army
Private First-Class Matthew L. Bertolino, United States Marine Corps
Petty Officer 3rd Class John T. Fralish, United Stated Navy

Flags 138-140
Lance Cpl. Billy D. Brixey, Jr., United States Marine Corps
Private First-Class Jason D. Hasenauer, United States Army
1st Sgt. Tobias C. Meister, United States Army

Flags 141-143
Sgt. 1st Class John D. Morton, United States Army
Cpl. Matthew P. Steyart, United States Army
Petty Officer 3rd Class Emory J. Turpin, United States Navy

Flags 144-146
Sgt. 1st Class James S. Ochsner, United States Army
Staff Sgt. Travis W. Nixon, United States Army
Private First-Class Joseph Cruz, United States Army

Flags 147-149
Petty Officer 3rd Class Fabricio Moreno, United States

Navy
Specialist Scott J. Mullen, United States Army
Staff Sgt. Troy S. Ezernack, United States Army

Following a brief intermission to check the safety of the
fire rings, we began with the presentation of Section VI of the
Flag Retirement Ceremony.

Section VI
Flags 150-152
Private First-Class Benny S. Franklin, United States Army
Sgt. 1st Class Moses E. Armstead, United States Army
Staff Sgt. John G. Doles, United States Army

Flags 153-155
Sgt. 1st Class James J. Stoddard, Jr., United States Army
Lance Cpl. Steven A. Valdez, United States Marine Corps
Staff Sgt. Robert F. White, United States Army

Flags 156-158
Sgt. Tane T. Baum, United States Army
Chief Warrant Officer John M. Flynn, United States Army
Sgt. Kenneth G. Ross, United States Army

Flags 159-161
Sgt. Patrick D. Stewart, United States Army
Warrant Officer Adrian B. Stump, United States Army
Lance Cpl. Ryan J. Nass, United States Marine Corps

Flags 162-164
1st Lieutenant Derek S. Hines, United States Army
Staff Sgt. Damion G. Campbell, United States Army
Specialist Blake W. Hall, United States Army

Flags 165-167
1st Lieutenant Joshua M. Hyland, United States Army
Sgt. Michael R. Lehmiller, United States Army

Private Christopher L. Palmer, United States Army

Flags 168-170
Sgt. Robert G. Davis, United States Army
Lance Cpl. Phillip C. George, United States Marine Corps
1st Lieutenant Laura M. Walker, United States Army

Flags 171-173
Captain Jeremy A. Chandler, United States Army
Sgt. Edward R. Heselton, United States Army
Specialist Christopher M. Katzenberger, United States Army

Flags 174-176
Staff Sgt. Christopher M. Falkel, United States Army
Gunnery Sgt. Theodore Clark, United States Army
Private First-Class Damian J. Garza, United States Army

Flags 177-179
Private John M. Henderson, United States Army
Staff Sgt. Michael W. Schafer, United States Army
Sgt. Jason T. Palmerton, United States Army

Flags 180-182
Chief Petty Officer Jacques J. Fontan, United States Navy
Staff Sgt. Shamus O. Goare, United States Army
Chief Warrant Officer Corey J. Goodnature, United States Army

Flags 183-185
Senior Chief Petty Officer Daniel R. Healy, United States Navy
Sgt. Kip A. Jacoby, United States Army
Lt. Cmdr. Erik S. Kristensen, United States Navy

Flags 186-188
Petty Officer 1st Class Jeffery A. Lucas, United States

Navy
Lt. Michael M. McGreevy, Jr., United States Navy
Sgt. 1st Class Marcus V. Muralles, United States Army

Flags 189-191
Petty Officer 2nd Class Shane Eric Patton, United States Navy
Master Sgt. James W. Ponder III, United States Army
Major Stephen C. Reich, United States Army

Flags 192-194
Sgt. 1st Class Michael L. Russell, United States Army
Chief Warrant Officer Chris J. Scherkenbach, United States Army
Petty Officer 2nd Class James Suh, United States Navy

Flags 195-197
Petty Officer 1st Class Jeffrey S. Taylor, United States Navy
Lance Cpl. Kevin B. Joyce, United States Marine Corps
Maj. Duane W. Dively, United States Air Force

Flags 198-200
Specialist Anthony S. Cometa, United States Army
Staff Sgt. Christopher N. Piper, United States Army
Sgt. 1st Class Victor H. Cervantes, United States Army

Following a brief intermission to check the safety of the fire rings, we began with the presentation of Section VII of the Flag Retirement Ceremony.

Section VII
Flags 201-203
Sgt. 1st Class Victor H. Cervantes, United States Army
Private First-Class Emmanuel Hernandez, United States Army
Sgt. Michael J. Kelley, United States Army

Flags 204-206
Staff Sgt. Leroy E. Alexander, United States Army
Captain Charles D. Robinson, United States Army
Private First-Class Kyle M. Hemauer, United States Army

Flags 207-209
Private First-Class Steven C. Tucker, United States Army
Lance Corporal Nicholas C. Kirven, United States Marine Corps
Corporal Richard P. Schoener, United States Marine Corps

Flags 210-212
Sgt. 1st Class Allen C. Johnson, United States Army
Specialist Robert W. Defazio, United States Army
Private Robert C. White III, United States Army

Flags 213-215
Chief Warrant Officer David Ayala, United States Army
Sgt. Major Barbaralien Banks, United States Army
Captain David S. Connolly, United States Army

Flags 216-218
Specialist Daniel J. Freeman, United States Army
Sergeant Stephen C. High, United States Army
Sergeant James S. Lee, United States Marine Corps

Flags 219-221
Master Sgt. Edwin A. Matoscolon, United States Army
Major Edward J. Murphy, United States Army
Chief Warrant Officer Clint J. Prather, United States Army

Flags 222-224
Staff Sgt. Charles R. Sanders, Jr., United States Army
Specialist Michael K. Spivey, United States Army
Specialist Chrystal G. Stout, United States Army

Flags 225-227
Corporal Sascha Struble, United States Army
Private First-Class Pendelton L. Sykes II, United States Army
Staff Sgt. Romanes L. Woodard, United States Army

Flags 228-230
Captain Michael T. Fiscus, United States Army
Specialist Brett M. Hershey, United States Army
Master Sgt. Michael T. Hiester, United States Army

Flags 231-233
Private First-Class Norman K. Snyder, United States Army
Staff Sgt. Shane M. Koele, United States Army
Petty Officer 1st Class Alec Mazur, United States Army
Flags 234-236
Specialist Richard M. Crane, United States Army
Sgt. Jeremy R. Wright, United States Army
Sgt. 1st Class Pedro A. Munoz, United States Army

Flags 237-239
Specialist Isaac E. Diaz, United States Army
Chief Warrant Officer Travis W. Grogan, United States Army
Lt. Colonel Michael J. McMahon, United States Army

Flags 240-242
Specialist Harley D. R. Miller, United States Army
Corporal Jacob R. Fleischer, United States Army
Corporal Dale E. Fracker, Jr., United States Army

Flags 243-245
Sgt. Michael C. O'Neill, United States Army
Specialist James C. Kearney III, United States Army
Corporal Billy Gomez, United States Army

Flags 246-248

Airman 1st Class Jesse M. Samek, United States Air Force
Corporal William M. Amundson, Jr., United States Army
Specialist Kyle Ka Eo Fernandez, United States Army

Flags 249-251
Staff Sgt. Brian S. Hobbs, United States Army
Staff Sgt. Alan L. Rogers, United States Army
Staff Sgt. Robert S. Goodwin, United States Army

Following a brief intermission to check the safety of the fire rings, we began with the presentation of Section VIII of the Flag Retirement Ceremony.

Section VIII
Flags 252-254
Staff Sgt. Tony B. Olaes, United States Army
Specialist Wesley R. Wells, United States Army
Sgt. Daniel Lee Galvan, United States Army

Flags 255-257
Sgt. Bobby E. Beasley, United States Army
Staff Sgt. Craig W. Cherry, United States Army
Specialist Juan M. Torres, United States Army
Flags 258-260
Specialist Julie R. Hickey, United States Army
Staff Sgt. Robert K. McGee, United States Army
Private First-Class Daniel B. McClenney, United States Marine Corps

Flags 261-263
Lance Corporal Juston T. Thacker, United States Marine Corps
Lance Corporal Russell P. White, United States Marine Corps
Corporal David M. Fraise, United States Army

Flags 264-266

Captain Daniel W. Eggers, United States Army
Private First-Class Joseph A. Jeffries, United States Army
Staff Sgt. Robert J. Mogensen, United States Army

Flags 267-269
Petty Officer 1st Class Brian J. Ouellette, United States Navy
Chief Warrant Officer Bruce E. Price, United States Army
Corporal Ronald R. Payne, Jr., United States Marine Corps

Flags 270-272
Private First-Class Brandon J. Wadman, United States Army
Specialist Phillip L. Witkowski, United States Army
Master Sgt. Herbert R. Claunch, United States Army

Flags 273-275
Commander Adrian B. Szwec, United States Navy
Command Sgt. Major Dennis Jallah, Jr., United States Army
Sgt. Michael J. Esposito, Jr., United States Army

Flags 276-278
Staff Sgt. Anthony S. Lagman, United States Army
Specialist David E. Hall, United States Army
Sgt. Nicholes D. Golding, United States Army

Flags 279-281
Staff Sgt. Shawn M. Clemens, United States Army
Specialist Robert J. Cook, United States Army
Sgt. Benjamin L. Gilman, United States Army

Flags 282-284
Specialist Adam G. Kinser, United States Army
Sgt. 1st Class Curtis Mancini, United States Army
Staff Sgt. James D. Mowris, United States Army
Flags 285-287

Specialist Justin A. Scott, United States Army
Sgt. Danton K. Seitsinger, United States Army
Sgt. Roy A. Wood, United States Army

Flags 288-290
Sgt. Theodore L. Perreault, United States Army
Sgt. Maj. Phillip R. Albert, United States Army
Technical Sgt. William J. Kerwood, United States Air
Force

Flags 291-293
Major Steven Plumhoff, United States Air Force
Staff Sgt. Thomas A. Walkup, Jr., United States Air Force
Technical Sgt. Howard A. Walters, United States Air Force

Flags 294-296
Sgt. Jay A. Blessing, United States Army
Private First Class Adrienne Barillos, United States Army.
Lance Corporal Bailey C. Spencer, United States Marine
Corps

Flags 297-299
Staff Sergeant Bryan E. Bolander, United States Army
Corporal William Amundson, United States Army
Private First-Class Kyle Holder, United States Army

Flags 300-302
Specialist Gianni Vasquez, United States Army
Sergeant First Class Tomas Avery, United States Army
Lance Corporal Marc Leeland Plotts, United States Marine
Corps

Flags 303-305
Lance Corporal Jason Barfield, United States Marine Corps
Sergeant Rick "Goose" Gossman, United States Air Force
Lieutenant Commander James Rodney, United States
Navy

Flags 306-308
Lance Fremd, MIDN, United States Navy
Frederick R. Minier, ENS, United States Navy
Brian L. Cardiff, LTJG, United States Navy

Flags 309-313
Frederick W. Caesar, III., LTJG, United States Navy
Randy J. Rickey, LT, United States Navy
Craig O. Reynolds, LT, United States Navy
Flags 314-316
James B. Brown, Jr., LT, United States Navy
James C. Radney, LCDR, United States Navy
Derek K. Christensen, CDR, United States Navy

Flags 317-319
Lance Corporal Gabriel Puchalla, United States Marine
Corps and Eagle Scout
LTC Kevin Kittrell, United States Army
PO3 Brandie Curtis, United States Navy, and Sister of an
Eagle Scout

Flags 320-406
All remaining flags were retired in remembrance of
thousands of other members of the United States Armed Services
who died in service to our Great Nation.

TAPS was played by the Bugler from Troop 1777, and the
Bugler from our linked Boys Troop 777. It was important to me
to honor the lives of our fallen heroes, while joining Gold Star
families together with others in our community to pay tribute to
them.

Together, we kept their stories in our present.

14 OVERWHELMED WITH EMOTION

When I reflect on the planning and development of my Eagle Project, I have one regret. My sorrow is that they have passed away and it gave reason for us to be part of the Gold Star community.

Pacing myself through my project was vital to its success. My notetaking for the planning took a toll on me. At times, I struggled to write the scripts for the dedication and retirement ceremonies. Every decision had a deepened significance because it was a reflection on these heroes. And that was overwhelming at times.

When I read their stories, spoke to their families, and sifted through photos of Jarrett, I felt a heightened sense of responsibility to embody their stories in all that I planned.

I didn't realize the gravity of carrying this load until I stood before the audience at the amphitheater on March 9th and listened to my older brother share Jarrett's story. I had heard it before. I had written the script. I knew every word. But this time, it was different. There was a finality that I still can't explain.

After years of assisting with my brothers with their Eagle projects, and participating in service projects for our Scout friends, I knew that challenges were to be expected. Sometimes there is a shortage of supplies or volunteers. There can be uncalled-for events, like stormy weather. I understand that obstacles with a project can test the leadership of the Eagle candidate. I had prepared, as much as possible, with a backup plan for hurdles that I anticipated.

I wasn't prepared to be completely overwhelmed by the emotion in that moment.

I began to sob on stage and the tears streamed down my face. While I knew that I needed to compose myself and return to the presentation, I felt lost.

Other Scouts stepped in to speak for me, and in that moment, I thought of Jarrett.

I thought of his super-cheese smile and a sense of calm came about. I made requests of my volunteers that gave me a few minutes to regain composure. They did an incredible job shifting some of their responsibilities so that our ceremony could move forward.

We continued through retirement of another 401 American flags. When the presentations concluded and the guests departed, I sat down and looked around as the fire rings were extinguished. I realized that after I wrote my final report and sent notes of thanks, that this project had ended, and I wasn't sure that I was ready for that.

Maybe, it didn't have to end?

15 A LASTING IMPACT

After years of Scouting, I was familiar with clean up after campfires. I knew that metal grommets would be buried in the ashes. I wanted to preserve them to give to Gold Star families who had shared the stories of their heroes with me.

The morning after the ceremony, I returned to the Amphitheater with my family. The grommets were carefully removed from the fire rings. Then, we used every container that we had for safekeeping of the ashes.

In the weeks that followed the ceremony, I led volunteers to make pendants from the grommets after they were polished in electric, rock tumblers. Scouts packaged the ashes into small jars that I would share with the loved ones of our fallen heroes.

I was registered to attend the Good Grief Camp at the T.A.P.S. National Seminar over Memorial Day weekend. I wanted to use that opportunity to deliver these keepsakes to others who were grieving like me.

I was anxious about the T.A.P.S. event because it would be my first activity with the organization. They had published an article about my Eagle Project before the flag retirement ceremony and a follow-up story was planned.

Most of the Gold Star community, that I had previously met, were parents who lost their sons and daughters. I didn't realize how many youths, like me, were receiving assistance from them too.

Following check-in at camp, I felt immediately connected to members of my group. Instantly, I knew these new friends would become a vital source of friendship and support. These peers were dealing with the same type of grief as me, and that was comforting. Mentors were there to be sure we had fun, while also providing a safe place for us to grieve together. The experience was life changing.

Camp included activities with NBA Cares, and we learned a few things from the Washington Wizards. I was sad when camp ended because we would travel back to our hometowns across America. I didn't know when I would see them again, though we promised to stay connected with video and voice calls.

My new friends had told me about their heroes. And now I am determined to honor them with ceremonies as more flags are placed into the boxes that were created with my project. This would be my way to continue to honor their legacies.

16 MAKING IT INTO A LEGACY

When I decided to paint silhouettes of fallen heroes on the box collection, I envisioned it as the best way to safeguard the deposited flags. The response in our community has been touching. I continue to receive calls when the boxes fill, and members of my troop hosted an additional retirement ceremony. Over 300 more flags have been reduced to ashes to honor fallen heroes.

My Navy brother, Noah, used the polished grommets from those flags to make a different type of keepsake for survivors- a paracord keychain.

Our American flag was designed with incredible symbolism that is woven into every star and stripe. I have found meaning in the grommets too.

A grommet may consist of two simple metal pieces. But it's the grommet that gives these flags the strength to fly. These pressed, sturdy rings allow the symbol of our freedom to remain on display until it was time to replace it. All made possible by the sacrifice of Jarrett and other members of our military who have died to protect our freedoms.

The grommet is a round circle that has no end, like the love that my family has for Jarrett and that other Gold Star families feel for their lost heroes.

These grommets have withstood raging flames of a fire. Once sifted from ashes and then polished into keepsakes, they become a token of strength.

While the rings have a hole in the middle like the one that was left in our hearts due to this incredible loss, the ring itself symbolizes the wholeness of our Gold Star community to support each other.

When I give grommet keepsakes to the families of America's fallen heroes, it is also a symbol of unity. It is my way of saying, without speaking a word, that "I understand" their loss.

Recently, my family buried flag ashes from the March 9th ceremony next to a Southern Magnolia tree that we planted at the entry of our church. Jarrett loved Magnolia trees. They reminded him of family trips to Louisiana for Mardi Gras fun and Cajun food. He and my brothers also enjoyed climbing a Magnolia tree at my grandparents' home in the country.

Rocks that surround this new tree are painted like red poppies- a symbol of remembrance and hope for a peaceful future. The color reminds us of the blood shed through their sacrifice.

Symbols have become an extremely important part of my healing, and I look for them every day. I know that my family and friends, who share in this loss, watch for them too.

I hope that my Eagle project will continue to have a long-lasting impact for survivors. I consider it my honor and responsibility to pass along their stories, to say their names, and to be sure our heroes are never forgotten.

Heroes like U.S. Marine Corporal Desmond Tyrell Watts, my friend Aurianna's dad. Auri and I met at T.A.P.S. camp. Desmond was a loving husband, father, brother, son, and grandson. He passed away at the age of 22. Desmond loved playing basketball, drumming on Guitar Hero, and being a dad to his baby girl.

Heroes like U.S. Marine Sergeant Major Jordan Johnson, my friend Sanaiyiah's brother. His birthday was the day after Jarrett's, but a year earlier. He passed away unexpectedly, during the same month as Jarrett and near the same base. His favorite color was red and he was a great big brother, son, and friend.

These stories connect us to something bigger than us. Saying goodbye to our loved ones is so hard because we loved them so much.

17 IN THE NEWS

My project has been the topic of several news stories for the past few months.

But it's not about me and it never will be.

I'm using my voice to say Jarrett's name.

I will keep standing to share the stories of our fallen heroes.

I will do my part to make sure they aren't forgotten.

When I was born, Jarrett wore an embroidered t-shirt that said, "Princess Grace's Security Team." It was a role that he treasured. He and my brothers often called me "Baby Girl."

On July 10, 2023, I became a Gold Star Sister. Honoring Jarrett is a mission that I will never take lightly.

As the youngest in our family, I am STANDING WATCH over his legacy now.

That is my pledge to Jarrett, to them, and to our world.

THE COURIER

OF MONTGOMERY COUNTY

yourcouriernews.com

SERVING THE COMMUNITY SINCE 1892

YOURCOURIERNEWS.COM   THURSDAY, FEBRUARY 8, 2024   VOL. 132, NO. 264   75 CENTS

AN EDITION OF HOUSTON ★ CHRONICLE

Jason Fochtman photos/Staff photographer

Grace Kotalik, a Scouts BSA member with Troop 1777, hugs her mother, Dawn, alongside her dad, John, after dedicating the final flag receptacle box for her Eagle Scout project in her brother's honor during a ceremony last week in The Woodlands.

SCOUT'S PROJECT HONORS BROTHER

By Sondra Hernandez
STAFF WRITER

As 11-year-old Grace Kotalik addressed her family, friends and fellow Scouts BSA members about her older brother Spc. Jarrett N. Kotalik, she wore a gold necklace with an inscribed gold heart pendant just inches from her own heart.

The inscription reads "Your

Brother continues on A3

Photos and mementos of the late U.S. Army Specialist Jarrett Kotalik. His sister's flags project honors him.

Bill Johnson, left, puts a bag full of American flags into a flag receptacle box alongside Richard Bolsey.

70

BROTHER

From page A1

wings were ready, but my heart was not."

Jarrett, 21, of The Woodlands, died July 10, 2023, while stationed with the U.S. Army in North Carolina. He was serving in North Carolina with the 82nd Airborne Division at Fort Liberty at the time of his death.

"Wings are so symbolic of him, that's all he ever wanted to do was jump out of perfectly good airplanes," said Grace and Jarrett's mom, Dawn.

About the project

Jarrett's legacy of service to The Woodlands community and beyond was Grace's inspiration for the Eagle Scout project she is carrying out.

Grace, a student at Deretchin Elementary, has created four wooden receptacle boxes where the public can donate old and retired flags until they can be properly disposed.

She dedicated the four boxes to fallen soldiers of Montgomery County, including her brother. Each box features information about the fallen soldier and the pictures depict things that were important to them in their life.

On Thursday afternoon, she held the dedication ceremony for the box dedicated to Jarrett at the family's home church of Trinity Episcopal Church in The Woodlands. The box will be placed on the church grounds between the sanctuary and fellowship hall as a way to honor her brother's memory.

Brother heroes

Grace is the youngest and only girl in the family. When she was born, her four older brothers, Reed, Rafe, Jarrett and Noah, wore black T-shirts with pink lettering that read "Princess Grace's Security Team," said Dawn.

As a kindergarten student, Grace wanted to be a teacher, and Jarrett and Noah who were in their teens happily played

Friends and family of Grace Kotalik, a Scouts BSA member with Troop 1777, stand for the Pledge of Allegiance during a ceremony where she honored her late brother, Jarrett.

along as her prized students.

The family's life of community service not only existed in The Woodlands, but beyond.

Community service

Dawn said Jarrett assisted with Interfaith, Meals on Wheels and showed appreciation to local first responders. When Hurricane Harvey made landfall in 2017, he jumped into action with his brothers and sister to make meals for families who had lost their homes in floods.

He helped with cleanup in neighborhoods, assisted at a Red Cross shelter for those who were displaced, and gathered food and supplies for points of supply distribution in East Montgomery County and Cleveland.

All of the brothers are Eagle Scouts with Jarrett obtaining the rank alongside his brothers on April 18, 2016. Jarrett joined the military at age 17 inspired by his great grandfather's story as a paratrooper who landed in Normandy in World War II. Noah serves in the U.S. Navy.

"Before his passing, he was a volunteer for our other brothers' Eagle projects," Grace said. "Unfortunately, Jarrett isn't here to assist with mine. Because he was deeply patriotic, I drew in-

The exterior of a flag box built by Grace Kotalik. She dedicated the final flag receptacle box, for her Eagle Scout project, to her brother.

spiration from him in my planning (for the flag donation project.)"

Someone at church approached her knowing she was a Scouts BSA member and asked where they could retire many flags that had been collected.

They were brought to the church along with others over time, and the church had no place to go with them so she matched a need in the community with her wish to honor her brother and the project was born.

About the boxes

She dedicated the first box on Jan. 26. It is dedicated to fallen U.S. Air Force member Cody Ball, who died in the United Kingdom in January 2023, and other Air Force members. She hopes to have the flag collection box placed at the Montgomery County Veteran's Memorial Park in Conroe.

The second box will be at the Timber Lakes Timber Ridge HOA at 25610 Timber Lakes Drive in Spring. This box salutes U.S. Marines and the U.S. Navy, and honors the memories of lo-

cal fallen soldiers Lance Cpl. Armando Hernandez, who died in 2021, and U.S. Navy member Kristofer Guy, who died in 2015.

The third box will be at the nonprofit Interfaith The Woodlands at 4242 Interfaith Way in The Woodlands. This box salutes the U.S. Army and the memory of Specialist Joey Lenz, a Willis graduate, who died in February 2023.

Grace made each of them personal with a silhouette painting of each solider on the front. Each box contains a QR code that will connect those who visit the sites to a website with more information about the project, boxes and stories of the fallen heroes that they memorialize.

With extra wood from the boxes, she made a plaque for the family of each soldier.

A personal touch

"I selected several elements for the box designs in remembrance of Jarrett," Grace said. "The blue reminds me of the Chicago Cubs, Jarrett's favorite professional baseball team. There are 13 stripes around the box. While that is also the number of stripes on an American flag, Jarrett always connected that number to me because I was born on Feb. 13. When he went through basic training, he wrote 213 inside his combat boots because he knew I was his cheering him on."

She will collect donated flags from the boxes and on March 9 will have a flag retirement ceremony at Camp Strake near Coldspring.

Grace is currently a Life Scout, the last stage before a Scouts BSA member becomes an Eagle Scout. With the completion of this project, she could obtain Eagle Scout status by late April.

Dawn said this will be a "legacy project" as they continue to assess the need for more boxes and maintain the current ones.

"The fallen heroes will never be forgotten, and in years to come everyone who visits the boxes will be connected to their stories," she said.

STARS, STRIPES, *and*

Dawn Kotalik ★ Surviving Mother of SPC Jarrett Kotalik, U.S. Army
Kristi Stolzenberg ★ Editor, TAPS Magazine

Service is something of a tradition in the Kotalik family. During WWII, a paratrooper with that last name landed in Normandy, and his legacy inspired future generations of Kotaliks to follow in his footsteps, including his great-grandson, U.S. Army SPC Jarrett Kotalik, who enlisted in the military at the age of 17. But, for Jarrett, his brothers, and his one sister, Grace, service started in childhood — pitching in with relief efforts after Hurricane Harvey in 2017, and pouring energy into their Eagle Scout community service projects.

Sadly, while assigned to the 82nd Airborne Division at Fort Liberty, Jarrett passed away on July 10, 2023. As the Kotalik family mourned the loss of their beloved son and brother, Grace turned to service, and through her Eagle Scout project, she found an outlet for the grief and pride she held in her heart for Jarrett. Drawing inspiration from Jarrett's service level and deep patriotism, Grace set out to earn the title of Eagle Scout in the wake of tragedy.

THE *Project*

Grace began her Eagle Scout project by building a flag collection box in honor

of her brother that featured her own artwork and details from the life he lived — all his favorite things. One collection box soon became five collection boxes — each a personalized memorial to another fallen hero — placed in key locations in Grace's community. Each box told the story of someone who bravely served, ensuring their memory carried on in everyone who passed by. The boxes also served as receptacles for U.S. flags that had proudly flown and were ready to be retired after growing tattered, torn, and sun-bleached.

By the numbers, Grace led a team of 92 volunteers — including fellow scouts, family, and friends — for a total of 1,777 service hours, across 50 service event days, and 708 flags collected for retirement at a series of ceremonies throughout her project, including the largest ceremony on March 9.

THE *Ceremony*

At the March 9 flag retirement ceremony at the outdoor amphitheater at Camp Strake, near Coldspring, TX, it was clear to all in attendance that Grace, with the support of her proud family, had given attention to even the smallest details.

From start to finish, the flag retirement ceremony ran three hours, with an 80-page run of show. The names of fallen heroes were shared as scout volunteers respectfully placed 406 American flags into fire rings to be retired.

The ceremony began with a moving presentation that replicated the opening of the Basic Training graduation ceremony at Fort Jackson, SC, where Jarrett graduated in January 2020, and buglers from Troops 1777 and 777 played taps during key moments throughout the event.

Several Gold Star Families were there to support Grace and represent the hero they lost. Grace took extra care to involve them in the ceremony and honor their loved ones. Kim and Carl Ball were there representing their son, U.S. Air Force TSgt Cody Ball. "Each Gold Star Family," they shared, "was presented a flag to be retired in their hero's name. It meant so much to hear our son's name spoken out loud with such honor." Their son, Cody, is memorialized on Grace's Air Force flag collection box.

After the 406th flag was retired that day, the ceremony concluded, but Grace's dedication to serving her community and honoring the fallen continued.

THE REST OF THE *Story*

After the March 9 ceremony, Grace and her team of volunteers preserved and sifted through the ashes to collect over 700 flag grommets, which she busily began turning into individual commemorative pieces for fellow surviving family members — including many members of the TAPS Family.

Since her March 9 ceremony, Grace has held two follow-on ceremonies to retire more

Service

weathered and worn U.S. flags from her community and honor even more heroes who bravely defended the flag through military service.

Grace's project bloomed into much more than a requirement to earn the title of Eagle Scout. By adding the element of honor to a very practical means of flag retirement, she kept the names of heroes present; she passed on their stories; and she brought surviving families in her community together.

"Our Matthew was honored and a flag retired in his memory," shared Milissa and John Guyon. "What a precious opportunity to hear his name and to stand alongside other Gold Star Families."

Surviving Parents Margie and Jeff Taylor shared. "It was so good to hear Joey's name spoken." The Taylor's son, SPC Joey Lenz is honored on Grace's U.S. Army flag collection box.

Joyce Fontenot, the surviving mother of U.S. Army PFC Trent J. Fontenot praised Grace's event, saying, "I'm so glad that I came. I got to hear Trent's name spoken out loud, and you know what that means to us. My heart is glad."

Grace made quite the impact in her little corner of Texas, and her impact reaches surviving military and veteran families

far beyond her hometown. The heart and personal grief she poured into her Eagle Scout service project was evident to all involved, including the board who reviewed her advancement to Eagle Scout on April 24. For all her effort, leadership, organization, patriotism, and community service, Grace Kotalik is now an Eagle Scout.

Grace proudly supported her brother, Jarrett — cheering him on in everything he did. Though he can't be with her now, she supports him still — telling his story, saying his name, honoring his military service, and using what she learned from him to serve others.

"Stars, Stripes, and Service" is a follow-up to the article, "Honor to Serve," published on taps.org in March 2024.

Are you interested in connecting with fellow military and veteran survivors in your community? Consider attending a TAPS Togethers event or TAPS Care Group meeting in your area for the comfort of TAPS close to home.

taps.org/tapstogethers

taps.org/caregroups

I AM A PROUD AMERICAN
by my brother, Reed Kotalik

As the bugle played and our family cried, soldiers saluted the remains of my brother.

When the American flag was placed into my mother's hands, I silently reflected upon its meaning.

The woven cloth of red, white, and blue symbolizes his sacrifice, honor, and commitment.

Despite the sadness over my brother's passing, I find his love of our country inspiring.

He stood ready "as a guardian of freedom and the American way of life" when he made his pledge, just three years before, as a soldier in the United States Army.

What a powerful message it sent that he was willing to pay the ultimate price for our freedom.

I am reminded of something that President Harry S. Truman once said, "America was not built on fear.

America was built on courage, on imagination and an unbeatable determination to do the job at hand."

My brother's service to America and Truman's words are reminders of what inspires me about our great nation.

As an American, I have the strength to be courageous.

It has influenced me to seek out ways in which I can contribute.

I find myself motivated to explore the wide range of freedom that is offered in our diverse country.

I have become resolved to connect with others to show a deepened sense of community.

As an Eagle Scout, I have seen people come together and make a difference in the lives of strangers.

I am inspired to continue that service throughout my life as an American citizen because I am free to dream, to speak, and to act.

America is the place that gives us a chance to do something different, to be creative, and to be innovative.

We have endless opportunities to create our own way of life.

My brother's sacrifice will never be in vain because he embodied his creed to always place the mission first, to defend our way of life.

That is something that I will always carry in my heart as a proud American.

I am prepared, more now than ever, to do "the job at hand" with making my own contributions to better my life and the lives of others.

I am a proud American.

PHOTO SECTION 1

MAKING THE FLAG BOX COLLECTION

PHOTO SECTION 2

INSPECTING AND PREPARING FOR THE FLAG RETIREMENT CEREMONY

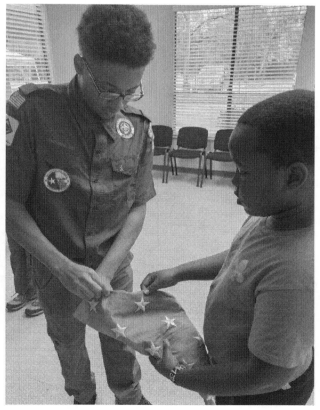

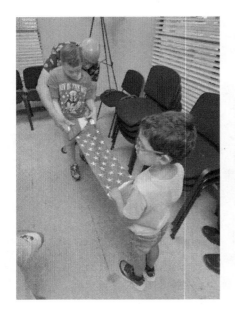

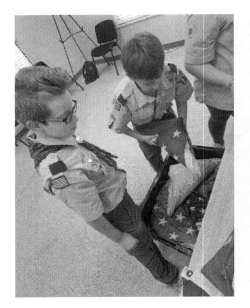

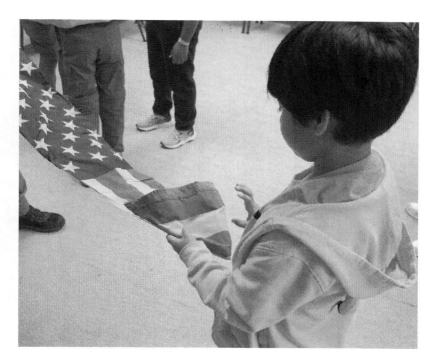

PHOTO SECTION 3

DELIVERY AND DEDICATION
OF THE FLAG BOX COLLECTION

PHOTO SECTION 4

FLAG RETIREMENT CEREMONY
AT STRAKE OUTDOOR AMPHITHEATER

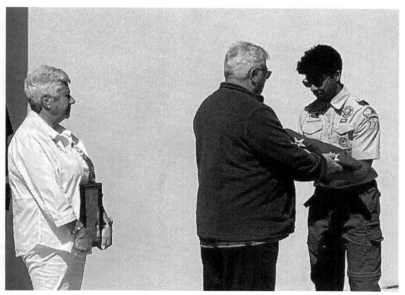

PHOTO SECTION 5
MAKING PROGRAMS, FLIERS, SIGNS, & SLIDESHOWS

PHOTO SECTION 6

APPEARING BEFORE THE MONTGOMERY COUNTY COMMISSIONER'S COURT

PHOTO SECTION 7

MAKING PENDANTS FOR
GOLD STAR FAMILIES
FROM THE FLAG GROMMETS

PHOTO SECTION 8

COLLECTING FLAGS FROM THE BOXES

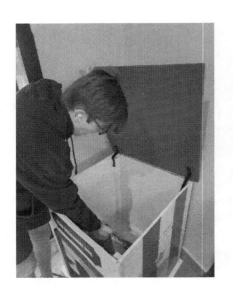

PHOTO SECTION 9

PRESENTING GROMMET KEEPSAKES
TO GOLD STAR FAMILIES

IN TRIBUTE

SPC Jarrett Kotalik

Fallen Hero's Hometown and State: The Woodlands, Texas

Branch of Service: U.S. Army

Rank: Specialist

Specialist Jarrett Kotalik served in the U.S. Army. He completed basic training at Fort Jackson, South Carolina in January 2019. He was transferred to Fort Sill, Oklahoma for advanced training in the Spring of 2020. In June 2020, he earned his Airborne wings and soon after became a member of the 82nd Airborne Division at Fort Bragg, North Carolina.

Jarrett was an avid outdoorsman. He dropped his line in ponds around his hometown of The Woodlands, Texas. His favorite fly fishing spot was in Cassville, Missouri. He fished in lakes and rivers in Louisiana and North Carolina. He also loved duck hunting and named his faithful dog companion, "Duck." Jarrett was a devoted fan of L.S.U. football and the Chicago Cubs.

Specialist Kotalik earned his Eagle Scout rank in April 2018, along with two of his brothers. He actively served his hometown within a variety of Service projects that benefitted some of the most vulnerable in the community. As a soldier, he earned several awards, including the Military Outstanding Volunteer Service Medal and Global War on Terrorism Service Medal.

Age: 21

Date of Death: July 10, 2023

SPC Jarrett Kotalik

Jarrett was the second oldest of five children. He graduated early from high school to pursue his dream of becoming a member of the 82nd Airborne, to honor his great-grandfather who was a paratrooper at Normandy in World War 2. His older brother is a Fire Control Specialist in the U.S. Navy.

Jarrett and his three brothers are all Eagle Scouts. He worked with them on many service projects, averaging at least 200 service hours per year as a Scout. His projects focused mostly on aiding communities after hurricanes, wildfires, and floods.

Jarrett served as a member of the 82nd Airborne for 3 years preceding his death.

Jarrett loved sports, especially college football and professional baseball. He loved attending college football games with his three brothers, younger sister, and parents.

lwalk4them
18 hours ago · 🌐   ...

Our next walk will be Wednesday, July 10, 2024. We will be doing two walks on the 10th. One in the morning and another later on in the day. Our first walk will be dedicated in honor of Army SGT John C. Barcellano, Age 26 of Ft. Bliss, TX. You will be able to read his story after the walk.

Our second walk will be in honor of Army SPC Jarrett Kotalik, Age 21 of The Woodlands, TX. You will be able to read his story after the walk.

www.iwalk4them.com

lwalk4them

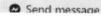

TIM FRENCH, DATE OF WALK: 7/10/24
CROSSVILLE, TN
IWALK4THEM.COM

SPC JARRETT KOTALIK, U.S. ARMY

Jarrett was the second oldest of five children. He was an Eagle Scout, like his three brothers and sister. Jarrett was active in service to our community and nation even before his departure for basic training. In June of 2020 and on the day after his 18th birthday, his dream to "earn his parachutist wings" as a member of the 82nd Airborne became a reality. Just three short years later, he would earn his angel wings at his base in North Carolina. He was an avid outdoorsman. His smile and his love for his family will never be forgotten.

THE SOUTHERN MAGNOLIA TREE PLANTED AT
TRINITY EPISCOPAL CHURCH, THE WOODLANDS, TX
IN MEMORY OF JARRETT AND OTHER FALLEN
HEROES

ABOUT THE AUTHOR

Grace Kotalik became the 6th Eagle Scout in her immediate family in April 2024, following in the footsteps of her dad and four older brothers who previously earned Scouting America's highest award.

Grace is a Gold Star Sister of U.S. Army Specialist Jarrett Kotalik, and Blue Star Sister of Noah, her brother actively in service with the U.S. Navy.

Grace has been involved with projects to benefit her community since she could walk. As her brothers planned and carried out service-related endeavors to benefit children and others in need, Grace would never shy away from the opportunity to assist. She has delivered critical supplies to the doors of families who lost their homes to flood waters. Grace has gathered food, books, school supplies, and medical aid for the most vulnerable. She has assembled meal bags for homebound seniors, made toiletry kits for the homeless, filled sensory kits for neurodiverse children, and crafted blankets for foster children. Her devotion to community has inspired others into action. Grace has been a Heart Hero for the American Heart Association.

Since the passing of her brother, Jarrett, Grace has become increasingly involved in projects that benefit our military and their families. Proceeds from the sale of this book will enable her continued support of non-profit organizations that serve U.S. Armed Forces members and their loved ones.

Grace recently became a member of the National Charity League. She is the current Vice President of Leadership for her Ticktocker Class. Grace is looking forward to expanding her philanthropy efforts in the community, through this affiliation.

Grace is an active member of her church and its ministries. She cares for animals as big as her horse, Sugar, and as small as her bunny, Hopper. While she believes a health-care profession may be in her future, she is determined to follow where her heart leads.

For more information about Grace's Eagle Project, please visit flagboxesforfallenheroes.com.

ABOUT THE PROJECT MANAGER

United States Army Major (Retired) Tammi Croteau has published over two dozen children's books and poetry and short story collections. This is her second project with Grace Kotalik, and she also worked with Grace's brother, Reed, on his two books. Tammi's passion for empowering young authors and illustrators to get started on the path to publishing their works has helped countless young people to share their ideas and talents with the world.

Tammi was the first female officer select to command the 319th Explosive Ordnance Disposal (EOD) Company, Washington Army National Guard. Now retired after 21 years of military service, Tammi now works as a Learning Management Officer for the Veterans Benefits Administration. She holds bachelor's degrees in Music Education and English/Creative Writing and master's degrees in Music and Emergency Management. She currently resides in Florida with her two cats, Maya and Briscoe.

Made in the USA
Columbia, SC
04 August 2024

39368425R00087